Imagine
...the fully devoted life

Leader's Guide

David Byrd

OUTCOME PUBLISHING
818 West Diversey Parkway, Suite W
Chicago, IL 60614

IMAGINE
The Fully Devoted Life Leader's Guide
by David Byrd

Published by Outcome Publishing
818 West Diversey Parkway, Suite W
Chicago, IL 60614
www.outcomepublishing.com

Unless otherwise indicated, Bible quotations are taken from
The Holy Bible, New International Version. Copyright ©
1973, 1978, 1984, by International Bible Society.

Printed in the United States of America

1. Religion: Spirituality General
2. Self-Help: Spiritual
3. Religion: Christian Life – Personal Growth

Contents

ॐॐ

Lessons Connected with the Imagine Book

Additional Follow-Up Lessons

Introduction

❧

This is a companion resource to the book *Imagine the Fully Devoted Life*. The purpose of this material is to provide Bible study curriculum to be used in a small group environment to teach the principles found in the *Imagine* book.

These lesson guides can be used in two ways. The traditional method is to conduct the *Imagine* study over a 10 week period coinciding with the 10 chapters found in the *Imagine* book. However, many churches are on a 13 week Bible study session schedule. Understanding this, additional lessons have been included to cover this period of time.

If a church is on a 13 week schedule, leaders simply teach through all sessions beginning with the Kick-Off lesson followed by Lessons One thru Twelve. The Imagine books should be distributed at the beginning of Lesson One.

If a church is on the traditional 10 week schedule, leaders teach Lessons One thru Ten while leaving out the Kick-Off Lesson and Lessons Eleven and Twelve. In this format, the Imagine books should also be distributed at the beginning of Lesson One.

As you look through the study material, you will notice scripture references to be read along with bullet points highlighting important teaching information to be shared in the small group setting. All small group students are also encouraged to read the *Imagine* book, answer the personal reflection questions, complete the evaluation exercises and spend time daily with God using the Quiet Time Guides.

Teachers are encouraged to allow time for students to share what they learned through their personal study using the *Imagine* book. Combining the small group experience with personal study has the potential to radically change those in the group. Enjoy the journey!

Kick Off Lesson
Remembering and Returning to The Foundations of Faith

કર્જ

The "World's Greatest Golfer" isn't always the greatest golfer. Tiger Woods has had to make adjustments in his swing. Why? Because at some point during his career, Tiger developed a subtle change in his swing, and the results meant that he wasn't playing his best.

> *Woods, who has twice overhauled his swing since turning professional in 1996, said the adjustment was relatively easy to make. "It was just getting back into my natural posture, which is no big deal," the 13 times major champion said. "That's what I usually play from, and you tend to get off. . . A lot of this is the same thing," he added. "I tend to slip back into the same old faults." (Reuter 9-13-2007)*

Too often, like Tiger, we can develop a small change in our spiritual life that, at first, goes unnoticed; but after a while this little compromise can influence our spiritual walk and life.

Hebrews 11 reminds us of the faith of the Patriarchs. By faith Abraham, by faith Isaac, by faith Jacob, by faith Joseph; the writer gives examples of these great leaders' faith in God, demonstrated by their actions and obedience.

When we come to the time of the exodus from Egypt we see a people who, over time, have allowed the influence of their world to influence their relationship with God.

ASK THE CLASS – What are some of the ways you have seen the Christian church influenced by the world?

Why do this exercise? By discussing ways the church has been influenced, members can recognize how their own lives have been influenced.

Remembering Who God Is

Read Exodus 3:13-17
- Three times in the passage we see the phrase, "the God of your fathers."
- God of your fathers separates God from the idols of Egypt. The Israelites knew the history of the Patriarchs and God. This emphasis was to remind them of their heritage and the commitment their forefathers had to God.
- The Israelites were influenced by Egyptian worship (Ex 32:1) Remember, they had been living in Egypt 430 years (12:40).
- Vs 17 reminds the people of the covenant God made with Abraham (Gen 15:18).
- Vs 18 Moses is assured by God that his message will not only be heard, but believed and acted upon.

ASK THE CLASS – We hear comments about America returning to God and Christian values. What will it take for that to happen? What is our roll in America's return?

Why do this exercise? This discussion question is designed to help each person realize that America cannot return to these values until the Christian individual makes the commitment to do so.

Tiger took some time off after his dad's death. When he decided to return he had some basic steps to follow. *Tiger said, "and I remember starting back -- anytime you take time off and start back, you always work on your fundamentals: grip, posture, stance, alignment. Well, that's what I learned from Dad." . . . "It was certainly a little more difficult than I expected," Woods said. "But also, then again, it brought back so many great memories, and every time I thought back I always had a smile on my face. As I was grinding and getting ready, it was also one of the great times, too, to remember and think back on all the lessons, life lessons Dad taught me through the game of golf.* (ESPN.com June 15, 2006)

Returning to God Isn't Easy

Read Exodus 5:6-9, 19-22
- Pharaoh didn't know the God of Israel so why would he allow his slaves to go worship this god.
- Instead, Pharaoh made their life more difficult in order to discourage them.
- The Israelite foremen curse Moses and Aaron for changing the relationship between Pharaoh and the Israelites.
- Moses questions God for Pharaoh's response, but note – Moses doesn't give up following God's commands.

Vs 23 – *"Ever since I went to Pharaoh to speak in your name, he has brought trouble upon this people, and you have not rescued your people at all."*

ASK THE CLASS – Read verse 23. How is Moses feeling? What are his expectations? How would you respond after the Israelite foremen asked God to judge your actions? Would you quit?

Why do this exercise? Moses' statement infers that he expected God to act quickly to end the suffering. This is to help us express the frustrations Moses had, and to realize God has a plan, we just need to stick with it.

Like Pharaoh, Satan is going to put obstacles in our way to keep us from committing ourselves to following Christ. He will try to discourage us from strengthening our fundamentals – sharing our faith, reading God's word, praying, serving, and tithing.

Realizing the Power of God

Read Exodus 14:10-12
- Pharaoh's army is approaching the Israelites. He had released them after the plague on the first-born, then changed his mind (vs 5) realizing he had released the slaves.
- Even after experiencing all of the plagues, witnessing the death of Egypt's first born, being urged by the Egyptians to leave, the Israelites begin to panic as they see Pharaoh's forces coming.
- Vs 11 & 12 will be a reoccurring theme in the journey to The Promised Land.

Read Exodus 14:13, 14

Moses' response to the people's cry of despair

- Do not be afraid – I'm sure this phrase could have sounded ridiculous as the people watched over 600 chariots bearing down on them, but Moses spoke the words with confidence.
- Stand firm – take a position, hold your ground. A military commander urging his troops to prepare for a charge in battle would use this term. Here the meaning could be interpreted as stand quiet/passive and observe.
- See the deliverance of the Lord – some translations use *Salvation* in place of deliverance. Either way, God is about to save the Israelites from the wrath of Pharaoh.
- The Lord will fight for you; you need only be still.

ASK THE CLASS – Why do we feel the need to "do something" or panic when challenges face us? What can we learn from Moses' instructions to the Israelites?

Why do this exercise? To help our members recognize that God can deliver us from every crises if we trust and stand firm.

Responding to God's Commands

Exodus 15:22-27

- The journey out of slavery and into a trusting relationship with God is beginning
- Vs 24 – "The specific word "murmur" (*lun*) or grumbled (NIV) occurs only in Exodus 15, 16, and 17; Numbers 14, 16, and 17; Joshua 9:18, thereby limiting the murmuring tradition to the wilderness era." (Reference: *Broadman* – Exodus p 378)

- Vs 25 – God's provision was right there for Moses and the people
- Vs 26 – God wants us to:
  o Listen carefully to Him
  o Do what is right in His eyes
  o Pay attention to His commands and keep His decrees
  o He will heal – Hosea 6:1,2
    ✓ Return to God and He will heal
    ✓ Torn/ heal references Deut 32:39
    ✓ We are restored to a relationship with God through Jesus

After the Exodus God used the journey to the Promised Land to reacquaint the Israelites with "the God of your fathers." They had to experience the power and provisions of God first hand. They knew the stories of Abraham, Isaac, and Jacob, but knowing the stories and experiencing God first hand is different.

We too, must be reminded of God's presence and promise in our lives. We can be numbed by the world. It is important to revisit the foundations of our faith and ask God to strengthen us.

As we have learned before, at the first attempt to cross over into the Promised Land, the Israelites' faith in God wasn't what it needed to be. Another 40 years of wandering was required to finally bring the Israelites to a place where they trusted in God and could be fully used by Him.

Imagine
...the fully devoted life

Next week, we will begin the 10 week *Imagine* study, utilizing the *Imagine the Fully Devoted Life* book. This study will revisit the fundamentals of our Christian faith: Testimony, Time, Talents, and Treasures.

Why are we doing Imagine? Just like Tiger needs to revisit the fundamentals of golf and work out the little hitches he develops in his swing, Christians need to revisit the fundamentals of our faith to strengthen our walk and service to Jesus.

What is our goal? Through this study we want God's Holy Spirit to make our hearts uneasy and restless about the areas in our walk that need to be strengthened. It is our hope that through this series we will rededicate ourselves to a fully devoted life in Christ.

Imagine
Lesson 1
The Assessment

৵৶৵

Begin by sharing your personal story about your spiritual journey. Include the following:

- ✓ Your upbringing
- ✓ Your first exposure to Christianity
- ✓ What led you to the decision to become a Christian
- ✓ What you have done to grow in your faith
- ✓ How you are spiritually different now than you were when you became a Christian
- ✓ What ministries you have been involved with as a servant
- ✓ The importance of your making financial investments into Kingdom work

These highlight the four areas of the Christian life that students will learn about during Imagine. They include their *Testimony, Time, Talents,* and *Treasures.* By sharing this information, you will be helping them understand the importance that each has had in your life. Explain that it is important to know who we are spiritually and to grow into the person God created us to be. We begin by getting a better understanding of who we are through an assessment. Read the introduction in the *Imagine* book related to the assessment and be prepared to give an overview of the information found there. Explain the focus of the four parts of the Christian life including your – *Testimony, Time,*

Talents, and *Treasures.* Have them complete the assessment found in Chapter One.

Explain that knowing who we are is the beginning of the journey. We need to grow from here. Imagine is developed in a way to help us accomplish this. Imagine is made up of four elements:

✓ Evaluation
✓ Instruction
✓ Reflection
✓ Connection.

We have just completed an **evaluation** element of Imagine through the assessment. Other assessment instruments will be used throughout the book.

You will experience **instruction** through reading each chapter. They contain specific teachings related to each topic which provide scriptural foundations and practical applications.

You will spend time in personal **reflection** by answering the "Q" questions which are found throughout each chapter.

Finally, you will experience one-on-one **connection** with God by completing the Quiet Time Guides which are found in the back of the book. Explain that each question on the assessment corresponds with a Quiet Time Guide. For example, the first question on the assessment is connected to the first Quiet Time Guide. The second question on the assessment is connected to the second Quiet Time Gide.

They continue to connect in this progression. Explain that they will complete 40 devotions, 5 per week for 8 weeks.

Spend time praying that God would change us and that we would become fully devoted followers of Christ.

Imagine
Lesson 2
The Story

ᕲᕗᕔᕕ

"On one of these journeys. . ."

When I was 16, my family went on our "last family vacation." We called it that because I was about to start working and it would be difficult to travel as a family. Mom has always been a "side seat driver." After a few days, dad finally got tired of her gasps and "Billy watch out" outbursts. He instructed her to stop the alerts. This happened just outside of Hershey, Pennsylvania. As we entered Hershey, we were all staring at the sites. Yes, all of us. Dad failed to see that the car in front of us had stopped. Yes, we hit it but not too hard. Mom said, "I saw her stopping." Dad looked at her, paused, and gruffly asked, "Why didn't you say something?" To which Mom replied, "You told me not to."

True story. *Teachers, use a story that happened in your life.*

Stories are important in communication. They keep us engaged. Everyone loves a good story.

TRY THIS – Have the class members turn to someone and tell him/her a story about something that happened to him/her. Give each person about 3 minutes.

Why do this exercise? It allows members in the class to get to know each other better and build fellowship.

Acts 26 – Be familiar with Paul's Story
Growing Up – Read 26:4-11
- Vs. 4 Paul begins his story by stating that the Jews, who want to kill him, know how he was raised as a Pharisee.
- Paul's life before his Damascus road experience.
  - o Lived the life of a Pharisees.
  - o Imprisoned Christians.
  - o NOTE – Paul did not try to make himself sound overly good, or exceptionally bad. He basically listed the FACTS of his life, letting them speak for themselves. No fluff just facts.

Paul was "convinced" that the life he was leading was the right life. Isn't that the way we all were before we encountered Christ?

ASK THE CLASS to share with the person next to them how they lived before Christ. What did you do, where did you live, how did you grow up, church background or not?

Why do this exercise? This is the first step to sharing our faith. Having the class members start here is good practice. It also allows other to hear the similarities or differences in their own stories.

Teachers, after the group has shared with each other, you may ask someone to share with the whole class.

Read Acts 26:12-16

- "On one of these journeys. . ." It was just a normal business day for Paul when he encountered Christ.
- Vs 13 about noon – speaks to Paul's zeal (Paul says "obsession" vs. 11) – unless a traveler was in a desperate hurry, it was customary to rest during the hottest part of the day.
- Vs 14 – Paul tells Agrippa the language that he heard.
  - Jesus speaks to us in our heart language.
  - Acts 21:37, 40 – Paul is requesting to address an angry mob
    - ✓ The Roman soldier is surprised that Paul speaks Greek
    - ✓ Paul addresses the crowd in Aramaic – the common language of Palestine.
- Just as Paul used the facts of his life before Christ when talking to Agrippa, he also spoke simply about his faith, not using any fancy language or words. It was (is) a simple message.

Kicking against the Goads – this was a proverb used by Semitic people and the Greeks. In training oxen to pull a plow, the farmers used wooden spikes to prick the animals' legs when they tried to break loose from the yoke. To kick the spike only brought more pain. The oxen quickly learned not to react by kicking, they submitted to their work.

Facing our Fears

ASK THE CLASS - What are some reasons we don't share our faith?

Why do this exercise? We must face our fears if we are to overcome them. By speaking these excuses/reasons out loud we hear our "fears" and often they don't sound as scary as we imagine them to be.

Have a volunteer read Psalm 56:3 aloud. We need to overcome our fears about sharing our story. Have the class repeat this verse out loud. It's always good to quote scripture☺

Read Acts26:23-29
- Festus asks Paul if he's nuts – not everyone will accept the message of grace. Many will offer insults
- Paul remains calm and does not waiver from his message. We too should stand firm in our belief and not back down when challenged. We may not have all the answers, but we need to show we believe what we know.
- Vs 27   Paul appealed to Agrippa's knowledge and experiences. In our conversation with someone, to appeal to his/her experiences or "emptiness" and relate our story with his/hers builds a connection. Both Paul and Agrippa shared a common knowledge; Paul uses this to link his story to Agrippa.
- Vs. 28 Agrippa's response to Paul is not clear to scholars. Some argue the king is greatly moved, while others say it was a "smarty pants" retort. In either case,

Paul's final reply reinforced his message and belief, and left the door open for further conversations.

Acts 26:2 Paul considered himself fortunate to be able to share his story with Agrippa.

We are fortunate to know the truth. We are fortunate to be a part of God's plan to share this truth.

ASK THE CLASS to turn to a neighbor and share their story of meeting Jesus. Tell your story like you would any other experience you've had. Tell the details: where you were, what was happening in your life, how did God speak to you, what made you finally say "Yes"?

Why do this exercise? So the class has an opportunity to share their story. This is good practice. There might be someone in your group who isn't sure of their story and this is an opportunity for the Holy Spirit to speak to them about their need for Christ. This could happen by hearing their neighbor's story.

Imagine
Lesson 3
The Purpose

𝕒𝕖𝕔𝕗

I Have a Purpose

Read Judges 6:11-15

We are introduced to Gideon. The Israelites have disobeyed God and He has allowed the surrounding nations (clans) to harass them. These clans are coming in at harvest time and stealing. To thrash wheat, you need an open area where you can beat the wheat and the wind can carry away the outer hull called chaff. A wine press is inside where the wine can be stomped and allowed to drain down to a reservoir. Gideon is hiding in a winepress thrashing wheat.

Emmer Wheat

The majority of wheat cultivated in Bible days was probably emmer, a type of hulled wheat. This is implied from the Biblical texts referring to threshing sledges and mortars. Hulled emmer wheat required considerable work to extract the grain, which may be the reason that threshing sledges were widely used in Bible times

---

Wine Press

Many of the ancient wine presses remain to the present day. Ordinarily they consisted of two rectangular or circular excavations, hewn (Isaiah 5:2) in the solid rock to a depth of 2 or 3 feet. Where possible, one was always higher than the other and they were connected by a pipe or channel. Their size, of course, varied greatly, but the upper vat was always wider and shallower than the lower and was the press proper, into which the grapes were thrown, to be crushed by the feet of the treaders (Isaiah 63:1-3, etc.).

When the angel of the LORD appeared to Gideon he called Gideon "mighty warrior." The angel tells Gideon, "The LORD is with you." (vs 12). Gideon's first response is "if the LORD is with us." NOTE Gideon changes the personal pronoun from singular to plural. Meaning Israel, not Gideon. The angel redirects in vs.14 and tells Gideon he's the man who will lead Israel. Gideon offers excuses in vs 15.

- My clan is the weakest.
- I am the weakest.

Vs 16 – The LORD answered, "I will be with you, . . ."
Gideon was just a man, husband, father, son, who was going through life doing the day-to-day tasks to survive. He discovered he had a greater purpose in life.

ASK THE CLASS – If you could have a dream job what would it be? Why?

Why do this exercise? This is an opportunity for your members to build relationships with each other by sharing a dream. It is also an opportunity for each person to think about a passion in his or her life.

Like Gideon, God has called us to a greater purpose, and like Gideon, we have to decide whether we are going to accept the call.

Discovering Our Purpose

Judges 6:23-27

Vs. 23 After Gideon's encounter with the angel he's fearful, but the LORD speaks peace to him, *"Peace! Do not be afraid. You are not going to die."* Isn't that how it is with us? When we experience God's confrontation of our sinful nature and accept his forgiveness, we experience His peace.

Vs. 24 Gideon makes an altar to God.

ASK THE CLASS – Why did Gideon make this altar? What are the altars to God in our lives today?

Why do this exercise? So that your members can identify moments in their lives when they encountered God and it was a milestone in their lives. The following are examples: salvation experience, a time of surrender, rededication, a commitment to serve.

Vs 25-27 Gideon's First Act as a Mighty Warrior

God's first assignment to Gideon was to destroy his father's altar to Baal. Gideon accepts God's command.
- Why dad's Baal?
  - It was the altar for the entire clan (family) including servants/slaves.
  - It was a small first step to experiencing faithfulness to God – remember God told Gideon, "I will be with you."
  - Shouldn't our first act of following God involve our family?
    - ✓ Acts 16:30-34 Paul and Silas witness to the jailer and his family.
    - ✓ Family is closest in our circle of influence.
- Why at night?
  - This is Gideon's first experience stepping out and trusting God.
  - Gideon is afraid. This is natural. He hasn't experienced God's strength in his life yet.

ASK THE CLASS - Identify any similarities in Gideon's reaction and action to God's command and ours as Christians. Examples could be as follows: following God can be scary at first, God moves us in small steps to grow us in our faith, we trust more as we experience God in our lives, if Gideon had not obeyed he would not have been prepared for the larger role God had for him.

Why do this exercise? Gideon saw himself as a nobody before his encounter with God. As he responded to God he grew as a leader. We want our members to understand that as they respond to God's command they will be prepared for greater challenges.

Summarize Judges 6:33- 7:25 by saying – vs 34 reveals God calling Gideon to a larger task. He summoned the Israelites together for battle. Gideon still had some doubts but sought God, and God confirmed His plan and Gideon went on to fulfill his purpose as a great leader.

Living Our Purpose

In the same way, let your light shine before men, that they may see your good deeds and praise your Father in heaven. Matthew 5:16

When you walk through a restaurant, most often you look at what others have ordered as you go to your table. If something catches your eye, you may ask the waiter/waitress to tell you about it. If it sounds good, you might give it a try.

NOTE – Teachers, if you have a story about this tell the story. Remember, stories create interest.

This is the same for our spiritual lives too. People should look at us and see a life that is appealing, be willing to ask about it, and to order it. People should want Christ because of our example.

Our Purpose is to Share

It's not enough just to live a godly life. Who led the most godly life ever? Jesus!

John 14:5-9a

Thomas and Philip have been with Jesus since the beginning of his ministry. They are disciples who faithfully follow his teaching day and night.
Both Thomas and Philip are confused. Jesus has to explain who he is to them and his purpose.

- *"I am the way and the truth and the life. No one comes to the Father except through me."*
- *"Don't you know me Philip, even after I have been among you such a long time? Anyone who has seen me has seen the Father."*

Jesus has to explain himself to his disciples. If He has to do this for them, how can we expect our "lives" to clearly lead someone to a relationship with Christ? At some point, we must tell our story.

Let's face the fears.

- "I won't know what to say." Remember, it's your story. Tell it like it happened.
- "What if they ask me something and I don't have an answer?"
    o What a great time to say, "I'm not sure. I'll look it up and let you know."

o Matthew 10:19,20 *But when they arrest you, do not worry about what to say or how to say it. At that time you will be given what to say, [20]for it will not be you speaking, but the Spirit of your Father speaking through you*

o Psalm 56:3 *"When I am afraid. I will trust in you."*

Imagine
Lesson 4
The Cravings

᷇᷈

This week, we looked at our "spiritual milk" and what spoils it. I Peter 2:1-3 says:

Therefore, rid yourselves of all malice and all deceit, hypocrisy, envy, and slander of every kind. ² Like newborn babies, crave pure spiritual milk, so that by it you may grow up in your salvation, ³ now that you have tasted that the Lord is good.

Here are some biblical examples of these "spoilers."

Malice – Ezekiel 25:3-7
God has told Ezekiel to prophesy against the Ammonites. They were happy when God's sanctuary was destroyed and the people of Judah were taken into captivity. Verse 6 tells us they celebrated with *all the malice of your heart.*

> **Aha!**
> an exclamation of ridicule (Ps. 35:21; 40:15; 70:3). In Isa. 44:16 it signifies joyful surprise, as also in Job 39:25

ASK THE CLASS – What are some examples of malice today?

Why do this exercise? By openly discussing modern forms of malice your class members will be able to identify if this is an issue in their lives.

Deceit – Genesis 27:34-36
The story of Esau and Jacob is filled with tricks and deceit. Here Jacob has dressed like his brother (including wearing wool over his arms), served young goats seasoned to taste like wild game, and lied to his old blind father so as to receive the blessing of the first born.

ASK THE CLASS – What were the results of this deceit? God had foretold (Gen 25:23) that Jacob would be greater than Esau. Was the deceit necessary? Why do we feel the need to deceive people today?

Why do this exercise? By openly discussing the reasons for deceit, our members may recognize that by trusting God there is no need to deceive others.

Hypocrisy – Mark 7:5-8
Jesus is confronted by Pharisees and teachers of the law and asked why his disciples don't follow the rules. Jesus responds by quoting Isaiah.

ASK THE CLASS - What is Jesus saying about the Pharisees? What are some examples of hypocrisy today?

Why do this exercise? By openly discussing modern forms of hypocrisy, your class members will be able to identify if this is an issue in their lives.

Envy – Mark 15:9-11
Jesus is on trial before Pilate. Pilate knows that the Jewish leaders are envious of Jesus (vs10). He also knows Jesus has done nothing wrong (vs14). He was not convicted of any crime.

ASK THE CLASS – Why were the Jewish leaders envious of Jesus? What are some examples of envy that we face today (careful not to let political answers i.e. class envy dominate)

Why do this exercise? By discussing "reasons" of envy our class members may recognize envy in their own lives.

Slander – Matthew 26:57 – 60a
Jesus is before the Caiaphas, the high priest and the Sanhedrin. They were looking for evidence to convict Jesus, but all they heard were slanderous lies.

ASK THE CLASS – What are examples of slander today? (if no one mentions half-truth, ask if that is slanderous and why?)

Why do this exercise? By discussing slander, our class members may recognize slander and half- truth telling in their own lives.

All of these "spoilers" that I Peter 2:1 mentions are alive and well in our world and probably our lives today. They all "spoil" our relationship with God and others.

I Peter 2:3 states "now that you've tasted that the Lord is good." Peter is referencing Psalm 34:8. *Taste and see that the LORD is good; blessed is the man who takes refuge in him.*

We are to be like God. When we are, people want Him and are more likely to take refuge in Him.

Last week we discussed that our lives should be appealing to others. We should look DELICIOUS. People should want to TASTE our lives.

I Peter 2:11 – *Dear friends, I urge you, as aliens and strangers in the world, to abstain from sinful desires, which war against your soul.*

ASK THE CLASS – What are some ways to abstain from sinful desires?

Why do this exercise? By discussing how to abstain from sinful desires your class members will offer suggestions that they believe they can do.

As we abstain from the "spoilers" of our spiritual milk we begin to reflect Christ in our actions. We look like Colossians 3:12-17 (Read this scripture)

Imagine the impact we as individuals can make when we live like this.

QUESTION FOR THE CLASS

Have you shared your story with anyone this week? Let someone share if they have.

Imagine
Lesson 5
The Disciplines

Start class by asking some simple math questions: 2+2, 6+6, 4x4, 6x6, 12x12 (this one's my favorite because it's the end!). Everyone was able to answer these simple math equations:

- Why? We learned them as kids in elementary school.
- How? We practiced them over and over again.

Now we are so familiar with them that they are second nature to us.

My son Phillip asked, "Why do we have to have homework? They already teach us at school. Why do we have to do it at home too?" Could the same be said about our attitude for Bible study and prayer? Why do we have to do this at home? We already hear it in our small group AND church. That's a double dose.

There is a reason we should spend time daily in God's word and prayer.

> *"The fear of the LORD is the beginning of knowledge, but fools despise wisdom and discipline."* Proverbs 1:7

Developing these disciplines of study and prayer into our daily lives draws us closer to God, and being closer to God allows us to live the full and meaningful life Jesus promises in John 10:10.

The Discipline of Prayer

"Very early in the morning, while it was still dark, Jesus got up, left the house and went off to a solitary place where he prayed." Mark 1:35

The day before, Jesus was in the synagogue in Capernaum, while teaching he cast out an evil spirit. His authority and teaching amazed the people so much so that as soon as the Sabbath ended, after sunset, they brought their sick to Simon's mother-in-law's house for Jesus to heal. What an exciting day for the newly called disciples and the people in Capernaum.

I imagine the next morning people are waiting outside in the front lawn for Jesus. Mom-in-Law is setting the table and asking, "Simon, go wake up Jesus, let him know breakfast is ready." Simon softly knocks on the door, "Jesus. Jesus, breakfast is ready." No answer. Jesus is gone. People lined up outside asking when Jesus is coming out. Breakfast casserole is sitting on the table piping hot, and no one knows where Jesus is.

Simon and the others find Jesus and exclaim, "Everyone is looking for you!" Jesus announces we're moving on.

ASK THE CLASS

- If Simon and the others could have made the decision of what to do that morning, what do you think they would have done? Why? (Jesus states in vs. 38 "let's go somewhere else" implying that Simon wanted to return to the town – don't you think the disciples wanted to stay where the "action" was?)
- Why didn't Jesus go back?

Why do this exercise? – Too often we make decisions based on what is going on around us. This exercise demonstrates that Jesus made his decisions by praying first rather than reacting to the events around him.

In his book, *Celebration of Discipline*, Richard Foster states: Of all the Spiritual Disciplines prayer is the most central because it ushers us into perpetual communion with the Father. . . To pray is to change. Prayer is the central avenue God uses to transform us.

Our prayer life tunes us in with God. As our prayer life goes, so goes our ability to follow God. In John 5:19 Jesus said, *"I tell you the truth, the Son can do nothing by himself; he can do only what he sees the Father doing, because whatever the Father does, the Son also does."*

The way to see what God is doing and what God wants us to do is to spend time in prayer with him.

"I Want to but. . ." Encouragement to Pray

Jesus instructed his disciples *"**Watch** and **pray** so that you will not fall into temptation. The spirit is willing, but the body is weak."* Matthew 26:41

In your personal study this week, you were given a chart to plan out a quiet time. Prayer is a discipline and requires discipline. We will be tempted to do other things we "think" are more important. Don't give in. Watch out for those temptations. Take the time to pray.

The Discipline of Study

> *"Do not conform any longer to the pattern of this world, but be transformed by the renewing of your mind. Then you will be able to test and approve what God's will is – his good, pleasing and perfect will."*
> Romans 12:2

What does it mean to renew your mind?

Last week we looked at the "spoilers," those behaviors and attitudes that spoil our testimony and relationship with God. I Peter 2:11 instructs us, *to abstain from sinful desires, which war against your soul."*

Read Matthew 4:1-11
Satan came to tempt Jesus when he was exhausted, hungry, and weak. With every temptation, Jesus responded with scripture - and when Satan twisted scripture to serve *his*

purpose, Jesus did not fall into the trap, but countered with SCRIPTURE.

ASK THE CLASS
- Why do you think our emphasis on memorizing scripture has diminished over the past few decades?
- Can we see any benefits to memorizing God's word in our lives today? If so, what?
- What prevents us from learning scripture?
- What would be an easy format for learning scripture? (a verse a week?)

Why do this exercise? We want our members to recognize that there are no "real reasons" for not learning God's word and that scripture memorization is not that difficult.

In a relationship between a husband and wife, best friends, and/or siblings we learn what to say or do to push the other person's "buttons." Sometimes we push them out of spite or meanness. Sometime we push them to see if it's still a "button" or issue.

ASK THE CLASS – turn to the person next to you and share one or two of your "buttons".

Why do this exercise? Often, identifying a button can help a person get "past" it. This also builds relationships.

Read Psalm 119:9-16

According to the Psalmist, learning God's word:
- Can keep our way pure.
- Can prevent us from sinning against God.
- Can bring great Joy like receiving a HUGE inheritance from a great uncle.
- Can bring delight – a feeling of accomplishment.

Knowing God's word can help us keep from pressing His "buttons." Our lives will reflect Jesus and a true Christian walk. We will experience joy and accomplishment. Most importantly, our lives will be appealing to others "by living according to your word" vs 9.

"I will not neglect your word." Vs 16

QUESTIONS FOR THE CLASS

Have you shared your story with anyone this week? Let someone share if they have.

Have you had your quiet time?

Imagine
Lesson 6
Passion

ഐ^ρക്ട

Describe a friendly church – smiles, says "Hello"
What's the difference between friendly and deeply loving?
(Deeply loving expresses genuine interest in getting to know others)

Why do this exercise? Examining the difference between friendly and deeply loving will help the class recognize that the latter requires a greater effort than a simple hello.

Our Attitude

I Peter 4:8-11

- *Above all, love each other deeply, because love covers a multitude of sins.*
  - Peter is instructing the church to go further than "hello." The deeper love is one that places interest in the well being of others.
  - *Love covers a multitude of sins* – this is a love that appears attractive to others. It's easy to pick out faults and sins, but when someone is expressing a deep love and concern for others, their mistakes are quickly forgiven and forgotten because their actions reflect a deep love and concern.

- *Offer hospitality to one another without grumbling.*
  - o Hospitality in this passage by Peter means friendly to strangers/aliens – this is part of how the church expanded, as missionaries traveled into towns and were cared for by the Christians. Peter wants them to welcome the strangers warmly and care for them.
  - o *Without grumbling* – grumbling is not a part of loving deeply. Grumbling is an act of selfishness. When you were a child, and you were asked to stop playing and take out the garbage, you probably grumbled. Why? Because you didn't want to stop playing to do a task.
- *Speak and Serve.*
  - o Our words and actions should be heard and seen as the words and actions of Christ. By the way we speak, act, and live we can attract others to Christ. They will see in us something different. By this, God, through our Christ like actions, will be glorified.

Our attitude towards others affects how much of ourselves we're willing to give. The more we love, the more we're willing to give up. This action of love and desire to give ourselves to serving others makes us, our church, and Christ very attractive to others.

ASK THE CLASS
Using a whiteboard, or large poster, have the class list all the ways they can serve others and glorify Christ. Group members will list ministries in the church, but get them to look outside of the church walls i.e. as a class - volunteer to rake an elderly neighbor's yard, volunteer to read at our Weekday or local school, make fresh baked goods for the

home bound's care-giver, establish a card ministry for the homebound – Police, Fire Department, local government,

Why do this exercise? We want the class to expand their thinking about serving. From this new ministries can be created. It's important to write it on a poster so the class can see/read it. This helps them remember what others said, and it generates new ideas.

Helping Others Connect

The Apathyville Horror
John and Susan were so excited about their idea for the church's college kids. Their idea would be to get their class to send the students a card of encouragement once a quarter. They could even host a Christmas or summer fellowship with the students so the class and kids could get to know each other better. Over the next few weeks, John and Susan would bring up their idea and suggests ways of starting it - but the class, though they said it was a "good idea," never followed through. Eventually John and Susan stopped talking about the college cards and the idea was swallowed into the abyss, known as Apathyville.

James 2:15,16
Suppose a brother or sister is without clothes and daily food. [16]If one of you says to him, "Go, I wish you well; keep warm and well fed," but does nothing about his physical needs, what good is it?

Look up apathy in the thesaurus and you'll see words like: indifference, lack of concern, lack of interest. Is this the way we are asked to respond?

Our willingness to serve is dependent on our attitude. If we have apathy, we will reflect it in our service to God and others. If we are moving towards a fully devoted life. our desire to get involved and serve will increase.

ASK THE CLASS
What causes apathy and what is the cure for it?

Why do this exercise? As our class members discuss apathy, hopefully they will discover where their heart lies.

You've heard the expression, "garbage in, garbage out." How about, "Love in – Love out." When we begin to serve others and express God's love, we begin to see even more opportunities to share the love of God. We also discover that it's not a chore, but a joy. It becomes a passion.

As this joy and passion begins in a few, it will spread to others. Not everyone will catch the change in attitude, but many will. The momentum of love and service will grow.

Marketing Christianity

Matthew 7:15-20

> [15]*"Watch out for false prophets. They come to you in sheep's clothing, but inwardly they are ferocious wolves. [16]By their fruit you*

will recognize them. Do people pick grapes from thorn bushes, or figs from thistles? [17]Likewise every good tree bears good fruit, but a bad tree bears bad fruit. [18]A good tree cannot bear bad fruit, and a bad tree cannot bear good fruit. [19]Every tree that does not bear good fruit is cut down and thrown into the fire. [20]Thus, by their fruit you will recognize them.

- People may try to act like Christians, but in the end, their attitudes will reveal their heart.
- Read Galatians 5:22 – The Fruits of the Spirit are – Love, Joy, Peace, Patience, Kindness, Goodness, Faithfulness, Gentleness, and Self-Control
- The attitude of Christ – the Fruit of the Spirit – separates us from the attitude of the world. This attitude is selfless rather the selfish.

Our attitudes, loving deeply, and passion to go further than "hello," reflects Christ in our lives. Our lives should be appealing to everyone around us. They should see the Fruit of the Spirit in us.

How are we going to express the Fruit of the Spirit in our lives?

TEACHERS – REMIND THE CLASS TO BE DOING THEIR HOME STUDY. THERE IS A GIFTS SURVEY (P140) IN THIS WEEK'S CHAPTER THAT SHOULD BE COMPETED BEFORE NEXT SESSION.

QUESTIONS FOR THE CLASS

Have you shared your story with anyone this week? Let someone share if they have.

Have you had your quiet time?

Where are you planning to serve?

Imagine
Lesson 7
The Work

ಎ⊷ಲ

I Am Part of Everyone

Nehemiah 2:17,18

> *Then I said to them, "You see the trouble we
> are in: Jerusalem lies in ruins, and its gates
> have been burned with fire. Come, let us
> rebuild the wall of Jerusalem, and we will
> no longer be in disgrace."* [18] *I also told them
> about the gracious hand of my God upon me
> and what the king had said to me. They
> replied, "Let us start rebuilding." So they
> began this good work.*

Nehemiah has returned to Jerusalem from Babylon. He
was the Cupbearer to King Artaxerxes. The king has given
him permission to rebuild the walls of Jerusalem. The city
and the walls were in shambles. God has impressed on
Nehemiah's heart a burden for Jerusalem and the desire to
see it restored.

ASK THE CLASS
What are some examples of "burdens God has laid on peoples hearts" that you have heard of? Has God laid a burden on your heart? How did you respond?

Why do this exercise? We want our class members to recognize that God does give us passions for different ministries.

Vs 18
- Nehemiah shared with the people his vision – how God opened the opportunity to speak with the king and how the king responded favorably.
- The people caught the vision and began the work
- Remember back in lesson 1 & 2 how we talked about how important our story is. This is an example of Nehemiah sharing a part of his story and the people responding.

The wall was rebuilt in 52 days. The entire wall was completed. The whole city was protected.

How did this happen?
- The people recognized God was providing.
- The people worked together.
- Everyone participated (except the nobles of Tekoa who refused to help 3:5).

Not everyone lifted stones and not everyone spread mortar, but everyone pitched in. Everyone contributed. Chapter 3 is full of "next to him." Imagine a church where everyone finds a place to serve and works "next to him."

Give Me a Hand

In your book this past week, you read Ephesians 2:10 and you learned that we are created to "do good works, which God prepared in advance for us to do."

I Corinthians 12:14-20,27

> [14]Now the body is not made up of one part but of many. [15]If the foot should say, "Because I am not a hand, I do not belong to the body," it would not for that reason cease to be part of the body. [16]And if the ear should say, "Because I am not an eye, I do not belong to the body," it would not for that reason cease to be part of the body. [17]If the whole body were an eye, where would the sense of hearing be? If the whole body were an ear, where would the sense of smell be? [18]But in fact God has arranged the parts in the body, every one of them, just as he wanted them to be. [19]If they were all one part, where would the body be? [20]As it is, there are many parts, but one body... [27]Now you are the body of Christ, and each one of you is a part of it.

ASK THE CLASS
What is Paul telling the church at Corinth? (the church is made of many parts). What is the most important body part? (There is not ONE most important part all have value).

Why do this exercise – The discussion is to help the class discover that the church body is diversified. We are not to be exactly alike, but we each have a responsibility.

- Vs 18 tells us that God arranged the parts in the body meaning:
  - ○ You joined the church because you felt this is where God wanted you to be.
  - ○ God has a purpose for you.
  - ○ We all have different abilities, skills, and gifts.
    - ✓ If the whole choir sang soprano there would be no harmonies.
    - ✓ If the whole church felt a passion for teaching preschoolers - who would work with the children, youth and adults.
    - ✓ If the whole church had great carpentry skills, we would have beautiful sets for Easter and Christmas programs, but no actors or singers.
- Vs 27 the body of Christ is very diversified and every person has a role to play.

ASK THE CLASS – how does someone get plugged in and serve in the church?

Why do this exercise? Some members do not know how to get plugged into service and hearing from others could encourage them to join in.

I'm Ready for My Close Up

Remember, God created us for a purpose – to do good works. As in our past lessons, our lives should be so appealing that others want what we have.

ASK THE CLASS – After you took the Discovery Test (p 140) what did you learn about yourself? How has God gifted you for service?

Why do this exercise? So class members can share what their talents and gifts are. By talking about them, they could feel more inclined to use them.

WE SERVE SO OTHERS MIGHT BE SAVED – Serving others is part of loving deeply (last week's lesson). This is an unselfish act that opens the door for us to share the love of Christ. Because we're willing to meet people where they are, they will be more open to hearing our Good News.

WE SERVE SO OTHERS MIGHT GROW – As we grow into fully devoted followers of Christ, we should be leading other Christians to mature in their faith. It's not peer pressure. It's guidance and encouragement, being willing to help our brothers and sisters in Christ to experience a fully devoted life.

We are God's workmanship, called to do good works. What has God prepared for you?

QUESTIONS FOR THE CLASS

Have you shared your story with anyone this week? Let someone share if they have.

Have you had your quiet time?

Where are you planning to serve?

What is our class's next service/mission project?

Imagine
Lesson 8
The Giver

ক্ষক

"One of the darkest days in American history was March 22, 1990. On this day, the President of the United States, George Herbert Walker Bush, declared in a news conference that: He did not like broccoli, he hasn't liked it since he was a little kid, and that he is "the President of the United States and . . . [he's] "not going to eat any more broccoli." In addition, the President also banned broccoli from the White House and Air Force One menus" (www.eatbroccoli.org).

We make choices everyday, and whether we realize it or not, our choices impact the lives of others. President Bush's comments were not intended to be a stern warning, they were given in a jovial manner; but there were still consequences. The U.S.D.A. reports that U.S. broccoli consumption hit an all-time peak the year before he took office and then declined by as much as 15% during his presidency" (www.eatbroccoli.org).

ASK THE CLASS
Have your members share with the person next to them some of the vegetables they have "chosen" not to eat since they moved out of mom's house. How is this vegetable "good for you" and how have you replaced its nutrition in your diet?

Why do this exercise? - We are building relationships with each other. We will also identify choices we've made and the changes we've made because of these choices.

The Choice

Read Philippians 4:14-16

- Vs 14 – The church at Philippi had a special relationship with Paul. They have shared in his troubles
- Vs 15 & 16 the Philippians financially participated in Paul's ministry, setting out from Macedonia and even in Thessalonica.
  o When other churches were choosing not to send aid, Philippi was choosing to help
  o The Philippians were faithful to give again and again to help Paul in spreading the Gospel of Jesus Christ.
  o Paul's effort was strengthened because of their obedience to give

ASK THE CLASS
How has the church helped to further the Gospel of Christ? How would our testimony be different if there was no money involved?

Why do this exercise? To help our members understand that we have a broader ministry roll due to our financial support.

The Changes

Philippians 4:17-20

- Vs 17 – "what may be credited to your account"
  o This reference is not about Paul's ledger
  o The gifts are used to further Paul's work for Christ
  o The lives surrendering to Christ through Paul's ministry are also credited to Philippi because of their support
  o Not everyone is able to "go," but everyone IS able to give.

- Vs 18 – Paul is thanking the church for the gift he's just received – they are continuing to support him.
  o He is amply supplied to continue on his mission
  o Their giving is a fragrant offering, an acceptable sacrifice, pleasing to God

Psalm 51:16,17
  - It's not the burnt bull that pleases God
  - It's the broken spirit – "not my will but thine"
  - It's the contrite heart – "I'm sorry. I want to be obedient"

The Philippians gifts are given from their heart. Given because they love God, want to see His message shared, and want to be obedient to all His commands.
  - Vs 19 – Paul understands that God is going to meet every need because He has been experiencing God's faithfulness of his needs being met in every situation. He writes vs 19 with confidence that God will meet the needs of the Philippians too.

- As the Philippians experience God's provisions they too will testify to His faithfulness, and once again, God will be glorified.

ASK THE CLASS
Why does God instruct us to bring the "whole tithe into the storehouse" (Malachi 3:10a). What are the changes we can expect when we begin tithing?

Why do this exercise? – We want the class to recognize that their tithe impacts God's Kingdom work. We also want them to realize, by giving to God, it gives them the chance to be BLESSED by God.

Group Activity
In your home study this week you studied four types of givers:
1. The Non Giver
2. The Partial Giver
3. The Whole Giver
4. The Over Giver

Ask your class members to turn to a person near them and "roll play." Beginning with Non Giver, pretend you are that type of giver and offer reasons for your position. Then both discuss ways to improve and how God will work to grow you in your giving faith. After roll playing the non-giver, move to the partial giver and so on.

Why do this exercise? – There are, possibly, all four groups in your class. This allows each person to express his/her "reasons" for being where they are, but also allows them _to discuss how God can help them move further in their tithing faith without feeling singled out._

In this past week, each person was asked to complete a current budget. If you haven't done this, please do it. We will not be discussing each person's budget next week, but it will help you as we complete next week's lesson.

Questions for the Class

Have you shared your story with anyone this week? Let someone share if they have.

Have you had your quiet time?

Where are you planning to serve?

What is our class' next service/mission project?

What kind of giver do you want to be?

Imagine
Lesson 9
The Margin
ॐ∞ॐ

ASK THE CLASS
What is the definition of being rich?

Why do this exercise? – Everyone has their view of what being rich is, by sharing these views the class will see different opinions. This will also stimulate ideas to be shared later.

CONSIDER THIS DEFINITION – Being rich is having enough to meet our needs and having enough to meet the needs of others.

There is a difference between being Rich and being Generous. Rich is having enough to meet our needs and others. Generous is giving of our surplus to meet other's needs.

The Giving Heart

Read 2 Corinthians 9:7,8
- We must decide in our heart what and how to give
  - Our giving reflects our heart or attitude.

- o Reluctant giving reflects an uncertainty in our faith that God will meet our needs.
- o Compulsion – definitions: *coerced, obligation, duress* is not the attitude that God wants us to give from – this is how we pay our taxes, not our tithe.
- o A cheerful giver is someone who understands that their wealth is not tied up in money or possessions. They give freely with joy because they want to be obedient to God and a blessing to others.

- ▪ "And God is able"
  - o to make all grace abound in you. Throughout chapters 8 & 9, Paul has been using "grace" and "blessing" as terms for material gifts meant for distribution.
  - o to provide for your every need – all things at all times.
  - o to bless the tithes and expand the harvest.

God is able to meet every need we have. Often, though, we confuse our needs with our wants. God wants us to be cheerful obedient givers. Generous. Our giving should reflect this: Our Needs, Others Needs, Wants.

> God gives to meet our needs.
> God gives so we can meet the needs of others.

After we have responded to the needs, then we can indulge our wants. Our wants are last. Our needs and the needs of others come before our wants and desires.

The Encouraged Heart

Read 2 Corinthians 8:1-5, 7

- The Macedonian churches (including Philippi, Thessalonica, and Berea) are under persecution from the Romans including the destruction of property and theft of goods.
  o They knew severe poverty.
  o They experienced abundant joy.
  o They gave according to their means.
  o They gave above their means.
  o They wanted to be apart of what God was doing.
  o They wanted to be apart of the blessing of others.
  o Their priorities were in the right place.
    ✓ They gave themselves first to the Lord.
    ✓ They gave themselves to support Paul's ministry.
  o Paul uses this example to challenge and encourage the church at Corinth.
    ✓ They excel in so many areas – faith, speech, knowledge, love for Paul.
    ✓ They should strive to excel in the grace of giving.

ASK THE CLASS
Why do you think the Corinthians needed to step up in their giving? Why does it seem that tithing is so difficult for us? How do we learn "God is able?"

Why do this exercise? – We want to identify why tithing seems to be difficult to do. We also want to acknowledge God is able to provide.

The Macedonians gave themselves to the Lord, His will. They wanted to help meet the needs of others. So, what do others need today? The Tithe. God asks for 10% of all He has provided to you. With that, He will meet the needs of others and bless the giver too.

The Focused Heart

Read Mark 12:42-44

The widow's heart and attitude were in line with God. She gave her ALL to Him; financially and submissively. She held back nothing.

Our lives should be the same. We should be willing to give all we have and are to God; we should trust that He will meet our every need.

10% - too often we look at this figure and see a large amount. After all, 10% of $65,000 is $6500; $100,000 is $10,000.

Ten thousand dollars sound like a lot. But think about it. God asks for $10,000 and leaves $90,000 for us. Which would you choose $10,000 or $90,000?

A budget helps us focus our hearts by identifying our priorities and responsibilities. Last week, you were asked to fill out a budget.

ASK THE CLASS
Who can tell us how a budget has helped their family
manage their income? What are some tips for budgeting?

*Why do this exercise? – There are members in your class
who've never considered making a budget. Testimonies
are helpful in encouraging others.*

Today you need to go home, pray, and fill out the NEW
budget column (p.161). Remember, examine your budget
and identify true needs as opposed to wants.

You need a car to get to work. Do you NEED a Porsche?
REMEMBER, there is nothing wrong with nice things, as
long as you can afford them and still meet the needs of
others through the giving of your tithe.

In our lives and in our budget, God comes first.

What if. . . .
Because of choices in your past or circumstances beyond
your control you cannot obediently tithe?
  o God wants an obedient giver. He knows your heart.
     Start where you are and move towards obedience.
  o Examine your lifestyle. Are you in debt because of
     WANTS or NEEDS?
  o What changes in your budget can you make to get
     you in position to be an obedient giver?

Questions for the Class

Have you shared your story with anyone this week? Let someone share if they have.

Have you had your quiet time?

Where are you planning to serve?

What is our class's next service/mission project?

What kind of giver do you want to be?

How do you plan to meet the challenge of a "fully devoted life"?

Imagine
Lesson 10
Now What?

ॐॐ

In his farewell address, President George Washington offered a warning stressing the importance of unity and the danger of factions:

> *The unity of Government, which constitutes you one people, is also now dear to you. It is justly so; for it is a main pillar in the edifice of your real independence, the support of your tranquillity at home, your peace abroad; of your safety; of your prosperity; of that very Liberty, which you so highly prize. But as it is easy to foresee, that, from different causes and from different quarters, much pains will be taken, many artifices employed, to weaken in your minds the conviction of this truth.*

ASK THE CLASS – If you knew you were leaving, and could give a final piece of advise/instruction/encouragement to your family and friends, what would it be?

Why do this exercise – Our final instructions often reflect what is most important to us. This exercise will challenge the class to discover what is most important.

Paul is on his way to Jerusalem. Paul knows he will never return to Ephesus, so he invites the leaders to meet with him one last time in order to encourage and challenge them.

Prediction of Persecution

Acts 20:28-31
Paul predicts persecution for the church.
- 28 – Paul challenges the leaders to keep watch over each other and the flock. Though this challenge is offered to the leaders meeting with Paul, all Christians are called to help each other live an outward Christian live.
- 29 – The wolves are coming! The churches of Asia minor will experience great persecution from Rome.
- 30 – There will be people IN their church who will *distort the truth*. A group called Nicolaitans tried to corrupt the church in Ephesus. Revelation 2:6 tells us that the Ephesians resisted (hated) the teachings of this group.
- 31 – Paul has passionately expressed his warnings and concerns to the church at Ephesus that problems were brewing.

ASK THE CLASS – How is the church persecuted today from without? From within? How do we guard ourselves against these attacks?

Why do this exercise – This discussion can help our members not only recognize the efforts of Satan outside and inside, but the need for us to work together to defeat his attacks.

Pattern with a Purpose

Acts 20:33-35
Paul is offering his final blessings and challenges to the Ephesisans before he leaves for Rome.

- Vs 33,34 – Paul wasn't lazy. He took responsibility for his needs and the needs of his companions. He wasn't interested in what others had, but worked for what his needs were.
- Vs 35 – Paul's pattern of living was a model to the church, an example of living out the instructions of Christ. Paul didn't just tell the church how to act, he lived his message, allowing his actions to back up his words.
  o James 2:17 reminds us that faith, without works, is dead by itself – Paul is showing his faith in his actions, but he also boldly speaks of his faith – Acts 20:27 combines the two – words of faith and actions.

Paul could say with confidence that others should follow his example. I Corinthians 4:16 *Therefore I urge you to imitate me.* The goal of these last 9 weeks has been to remind us of, and encourage us in, the fundamentals of our faith: Testimony, Time with God, Talents, and Treasures.

The goal is for each person to grow in practicing these fundamentals and to help others along the way. Just like Paul predicted to Ephesus, we will face persecution living our faith. Satan will challenge us with each step of faith. Satan will tell you:

- "You will lose this friend if you talk to them about Jesus."
- "You don't have time to read the Bible right now, maybe later." "Say your prayers after you get your work done."
- "You don't have any talents to offer the church. There are more talented people than you already serving. Just sit and don't draw attention or embarrass yourself."
- "You can't afford to tithe. You have bills to pay and you need the new HD TV."

ASK THE CLASS
What are ways we can continue to strengthen these fundamentals and encourage others in our group?

Why do this exercise – It is through being in a group that we have the best chance to keep practicing the fundamentals we've learned and to encourage our church to live it daily.

Chapter 10 in their Imagine book includes the same Spiritual Assessment Test that was taken in the beginning of the book. Have the class retake the test. Have them compare the results of the two assessments that were taken.

ASK THE CLASS – what have you learned about yourself? How have you changed through the Imagine journey?

Explain that the remaining lessons are for the purpose of assisting them as they continue to grow as disciples. Although the Imagine book material is completed, these lessons instill the discipline of Bible study and personal application as we become more like Christ.

Take time and pray, asking God to help them live out their faith.

Imagine
Lesson 11
With Thanksgiving
and Praise

ॐॐ

I have a Thanksgiving memory that will be with me forever. My family and my brother in law's family had gathered together for Thanksgiving. Both my dad and my brother in law's dad were pastors and had known each other for decades.

As our families sat at the table feasting, I noticed that my family was sharing stories about our childhood, vacations, exciting events in the Byrd family's life; all accented with laughter and tears of joy. My bother in law's family, enjoyed the stories and laughter, but didn't have many stories of their own to share.

Later, Jennifer and I were discussing the evening and she remarked, "They have stories, they just don't tell them enough to remember them."

The Jewish form of education was based on telling stories over and over so they would be remembered.

Deuteronomy 6:4-7 states:

> *Hear, O Israel: The LORD our God, the LORD is one.[5] Love the LORD your God with all your heart and with all your soul and with all your strength. [6] These commandments that I give you today are to be upon your hearts. [7] Impress them on your children. Talk about them when you sit at home and when you walk along the road, when you lie down and when you get up.*

The more we tell the stories, the better we remember them. The more we talk about the blessings given by God, the more we are aware of all that God has blessed us with.

Background

Read Psalm 105, I Chronicles 16:1-36

King David composed this psalm. The first 15 verses were used as a hymn at the carrying up of the ark from the house of Obededom. It describes the history and movement of the Lord's people and his protection and care over them. The psalm has four parts: 1-7 joyful praise to God, 8-15 the birth of a nation with a covenant with Abraham, 16-23 going into Egypt, the exodus and God's deliverance, finally 24-38 God's provisions in the wilderness and the Promised Land.

Vs 1 – This verse sets the text for the entire psalm.
- Give thanks to the Lord – acknowledges that it is God who has provided for us.

- Call on His name – He is the God of Israel and ours today There is no other name or god to call out to. Our faithfulness and allegiance is only to Him.
- Make known among the nations. Even in the Old Testament there is a command to spread the message of God. Joshua 2:8-12 has Rahab recounting the stories of God's power to the spies before the battle of Jericho.
  o The testimony of Israel had people "melting in fear"
  o Vs 11"When we heard of it, our hearts melted . . ."

When we acknowledge God and give Him the sole credit and praise, that testimony can change the hearts of others.

ASK THE CLASS – Share some testimonies of thanksgiving of God that are at work in their lives.

Why do this exercise – Like the Jewish education, we need to talk about God at work in our lives. The more we talk about it, the easier it is to share it as a testimony to the lost.

Vs 2   Sing to him – C.H. Spurgeon, a highly influential pastor – known as the "Prince of Preachers" said, "Bring your best thoughts and express them in the best language to the sweetest sounds. Take care that your singing is ' unto Him,' and not merely for the sake of the music or to delight the ears of others."

- When the Israelites were delivered from the Egyptian army they sang
- Before Moses died he gave a song to the Israelites to help them remember God's provisions and faithfulness so they would not go astray (they obviously didn't sing it enough)

- There are many examples of people singing songs of celebration and praise
- The psalms tell us to "Sing to the Lord" a new song – Ps 33:3, 96:1, 98:1
- They are to sing to Him and remember His acts and deeds

Music and songs were used to express the emotions of the heart, songs of thanksgiving and praise. Songs were also used as a means of teaching and instructing.

Vs 3   Glory in His holy name.
- Pride themselves in His name.
- Make it a matter of joy that you have an awesome God.
- There is no shame in the name of God. Let the hearts rejoice.
- The people of God should have joyous hearts.
- There should be a joyous anticipation in seeking God.
- To be able to seek after God is joyous.

ASK THE CLASS – How can we sing praises and glory in His holy name in our lives today. How do we sing and glory in the Lord's name outside of Sunday?

Why do this exercise? To help the class discover that our praises and thanksgivings should go beyond the classroom and worship center and into our everyday lives.

Vs 4   Look to the Lord and His strength
- Place yourself under the protection of God
- Protection can be a reference to the Ark of the Covenant that David is returning to Jerusalem
- Turn to God for His strength always

ASK THE CLASS – What are ways God protects us today?

Why do this exercise – to help the class identify the power of God in our daily lives.

Vs. 5   Remember the wonders He has done, his miracles, and the judgments He pronounced.
- David is reminding the Israelites again to not forget what God has done for His people.
- Keeping these memories – wonders, miracles, and judgments - will help keep the Israelites faith strong.
- Recognize the mighty acts and the results of them.

This verse encourages the people to focus on the blessings fulfilled by God - His wonders, miracles, and judgments - so that they can remain strong in their faith. When they stopped focusing on God and remembering His works, they moved away from Him and their Lord.

ASK THE CLASS – Name some of the wonders and miracles you've experienced or have been witness to.

Why do this exercise? So the class can identify the power of God at work around them.

This Psalm begins by telling the reader to give thanks to the Lord. We have discussed:

- Testimonies of thanksgiving from God,
- How to be joyous in our daily lives because of the blessing of God
- The protection of God in our lives today
- The wonders and miracles of God in our lives

It is important for us to remember and share these wonders when we gather together. These stories of God at work encourage us and embolden us in our faith.

Challenge the class – When you're with a group and someone asks for a "Praise report," don't sit and wait for someone else to speak. Speak out and offer a report of Thanksgiving and Praise about the God who meets all of our needs.

Imagine
Lessons 12
Live In the Presence
of God
～⸙～

My wife had the opportunity to interview for an Assistant Principal's position. She had a list of "possible questions" that could be asked. One of those questions had to do with her thoughts on the qualities of a principal.

We listed several things - good listener, approachable, educator, organized, and so on. As we read over the list, Karla said aloud, "Integrity." The Principal can have all these other leadership skills, but without integrity there is no value in his/her abilities.

Merriam-Webster's online dictionary gives this definition:

Integrity

- Firm adherence to a code of especially moral or artistic values: Incorruptibility
- An unimpaired condition: Soundness
- The quality or state of being complete or undivided: Completeness

Synonyms - Honesty

Read Psalm 15
In this psalm the question is asked who can be in the presence of God. From there the psalmist begins to offer a list of requirements for a person to be in God's presence. This list is not ceremonial tasks, but rather a heart check; revealing that actions and attitude have more to do with being in the presence of God rather than ceremonial cleansings and sacrifices. Psalm 51 reinforces this thought:

> *You do not delight in sacrifice, or I would bring it; you do not take pleasure in burnt offerings. [17]The sacrifices of God are a broken spirit; a broken and contrite heart, O God, you will not despise.*

Question

Vs 1 – David opens this psalm by asking two questions
- Who may dwell in your sanctuary? (tent - KJV) This first question begins by asking who can visit God in His sanctuary. This is not the Temple. Solomon builds it. This is still the tent - 2 Samuel 7:5,6, 12,13
- "Who may live on your holy hill?" David has advanced the question from visiting the sanctuary to living in the presence of God.

Answer

Vs 2 – begins the answer to David's questions.
- The answer begins with elements of Integrity.
- Walk, does, and speaks are continuous actions – who is walking, who is doing, who is speaking. So it is the person who is doing what is righteous and speaking the truth that qualifies to dwell in the sanctuary and live on the holy hill.
- Blameless, righteous, and truth all are heart actions. Our actions reflect what is in our heart – Matthew 15:17-19.

Vs 3 – the answer continues with what we say.
- No slander on his tongue – a reference to gossip and malicious comments.
- Does his neighbor no wrong and casts no slur – being mindful that our words hurt and once they are said they cannot be taken back.
  o It's said that the worst kind of hurt is church hurt, because they are the people you fellowship and worship with, this closeness is easily broken with words.
  o A slur, or malicious comment can cause others to create a negative opinion of someone.

Vs 4 – despises a vile man but honors those who fear God
- The next requirement (third) deals with awareness
- Being able to discern good from bad – Parents use this discernment when they meet some of their children's friends; warning their children "That kid's trouble, you shouldn't hang around him."
- Honoring (respecting) those who fear the Lord

Vs 4 – who keeps his oath even when it hurt. This, too, is a requirement for dwelling and living in the presence of God
- Deuteronomy 23:21 - [21] *If you make a vow to the LORD your God, do not be slow to pay it, for the LORD your God will certainly demand it of you and you will be guilty of sin.*

Vs 5 – the fifth and final requirement involved money
- Exodus 22:25 If you lend money to one of my people among you who is needy, do not be like a moneylender; charge him no interest.
  - Literal translation "He does not give out money at a bite."
  - Refers to exorbitant interest
  - *In Babylon, e.g. interest rates on money were often 20%; on crops, $33^{1/3}$ %* (G.A. Barrois, "Debt, Debtor," IDB I, 809)
- Taking a bribe does not reflect a life of integrity or a heart that reflects God

Affirmation

Vs 5c – He who does these things will never be shaken
- The person who lives this way will have a solid foundation with/in God

Psalm 15 could be an entrance liturgy or perhaps a responsive reading with the priest or perhaps a layperson asking the question (vs 1) and the congregation responding (vs 2-5)

The psalm has an immediate and apparent relevance to any who desire the Presence of God and are concerned to know what He expects. Its simple but demanding requirements are not dissimilar to our Lord's expectations of His disciples. They are stark reminders of what the faithful are asked to be, and an embarrassing description of what we somehow so seldom are. (Broadman Bible Commentary Volume 4 p.197)

This list, offered by the psalmist, should be what Christians aspire to today. Christian, the title, has lost its meaning in our world today. At one time, a person claiming to be a Christian was considered honorable, respectful, a person of integrity; now those attributes are no longer associated with the title.

The challenge for us is to live in the presence of God in every part of our lives. Being mindful that God is always with us, our lives should reflect these attributes of the psalm at all times.

As individuals, we may never change the world, but we can change the way those around us view Christians.

Notes

❧❦

Kick Off

Notes

༺∽༻

Lesson One – The Assessment

Notes

Lesson Two – The Story

Notes

❧≈❧

Lesson Three – The Purpose

Notes

❧❧

Lesson Four – The Cravings

Notes

❧❦

Lesson Five – The Disciplines

Notes

ം⸙ം

Lesson Six – Passion

Notes

❧❧

Lesson Seven – The Work

Notes

❧

Lesson Eight – The Giver

Notes

❧

Lesson Nine – The Margin

Notes

༺∽∾༻

Lesson Ten – Now What?

Notes

❦

Lesson Eleven – With Thanksgiving and Praise

Notes

৵৹৻

Lesson Twelve – Live in the Presence of God